Words of Inspiration from Your Own Kind

RACHEL GREER

authorHOUSE®

AuthorHouse™
1663 Liberty Drive
Bloomington, IN 47403
www.authorhouse.com
Phone: 1-800-839-8640

First published by AuthorHouse 04/29/2011

ISBN: 978-1-4567-3804-4 (sc)
ISBN: 978-1-4567-3803-7 (hc)
ISBN: 978-1-4567-3802-0 (e)

Library of Congress Control Number: 2011904894

Printed in the United States of America

Dedication

This book is dedicated to every person who thought they could not win. Dedication to those who that are ambitious, the ones that go hard!

This book is dedicated to every person who didn't accept no for an answer. To every person who stood strong no matter what was wrong.

This book is dedicated to every person that's not afraid to walk alone or on their own.

This book is the dedication to the ones that will rise again and again. I thank you!

I also want to dedicate this for all those who are trying, it isn't easy always and I understand that.

I dedicate this book to the struggle and the hustle.

I dedicate this book to all kind and every kind. I dedicate this book to my family.

I dedicate this to my brothers and sisters, you're lovely altogether.

I dedicate this book to all who support me.

Acknowledgement

I love to thank God for helping me realize the gift that I have. How tremendous! I would love to thank my supporters for unconditional support. Dad, you're so real and you're the greatest. Raven, Timeka Parker, Hailie, Lashunda, DeOne Jones (Thanks for all the NYC insight), Heidi (Thanks so much), Ashley(Keep your head up), Dynasty, Dymonique (May life bring you all of the best), M'Zariyah, Tamara, Chelsy, Jason (I feel you'll have the best urban book of all time. Impressive and very strong message), Edna, Gabrielle (you're like a big sister I never had), Marquon (Always love from me and that's for life), Desmond & Dareuss (The best male friends ever), Mama, Ms. Greenlee, Shy, Auntie Renee, Neosha (Stay Inspired), Perry(Man of Steel), Auntie Kathy, Pat, Sandra, Joyce, Keona, Danyale, Dawncia, Pam(you're 18 right) and Leon. Cece and Camille y'all always show major love and just know it's much appreciated. Tupac, I can appreciate your music, though change takes time, hopefully I'm making you proud as I stand strong as an african american woman. Rest In Peace. Aliesa Nicole, I know you're not a back up chick; we're not going for that; so hopefully we'll meet at the top someday. Swiss Money magazine for promoting my book and so much love to Derrick (Devise Graphics LLC), he's the truth when it comes down to resource. You're much appreciated and I support you forever percent with all your talents! Author Nicole Smith, thanks for all the advice. I'm very grateful! Anyone I may have forgot, I apologize but you're support is much appreciated.

Sponsors, I want to thank you all. Your donations are much appreciated and honored. It means a lot to have those certain people that help you get your dreams accomplished. Thank you so much.

Judy Taylor
Willie Taylor
Leon Gray
Doris Triggs
Ceceila Gray
Cousin Camille (all smiles)
Rachel Greer

Contents

Preface

What is it that has influenced my life? Indeed my life is fulfilled with various influences. Sometimes you don't always have someone who wants you to do well or even someone who congratulates you, so you have to be your own influence or even look for influences. In some cases you even have to see others and realize that's not what you want for yourself. In my case there are various influences in my life, but two are the most outstanding. Confucious and I are definitely the most outstanding influences I have in my life. Confucious has one amazing quote that's stuck to my brain like glue which is, **"Our greatest glory is not in never falling, but in rising every time we fall."** Those are such beautiful words that I abide by and live by. Sometimes people think about how bad they're doing versus the good they're accomplishing. Instead of thinking all of all life's problems, think of all life's successes. One thing that is for sure is whenever I do feel down, I find a way to raise my spirits up again even if it's just remembering Confucious prestigious quote. The quote is so uplifting and inspiring; it makes you feel like you can overcome no matter what. I am my own inspiration. I get inspired off the negativity of those telling me what I cannot be. I get inspired off seeing what others are and knowing someday that could be me. Even seeing my own potential, knowing that I was put on this Earth for a purpose, I have to be all I can. One thing that is for sure is, even in my worst fears or deepest scares. I still can overcome and uplift myself. One thing about me is I'm naturally ambitious so even if I have to stand alone, I will make it and be what I set out to be. Even when those haters look down on me, I'm proving them wrong by keeping my head up and keeping a smile. When I say to myself no matter what, I will still stand. I mean it, I told myself I am somebody. I will leave a mark that cannot be erased. I will do that because I'm that true to my word.

Was It That Easy?

To hurt me like that
To lie to me so damn much
To cheat so openly
To embarrass me
To harass me
To fall out of love
To make me believe it was you and me
To tell me you love me
To tell me you are gonna be committed
To make an excuse for the lies you submitted
To hide so many things from me
To pretend like you were the one
To call me a bitch and not give a damn
To just let our love vanish
To hit me over and over again
To kill me with those words
To risk me
To take me for granted
To be so selfish
Was it that easy?

So Beautiful

That I go to bed with you by my side
That I wake up to your smelly breath
That I make you breakfast and off to work we go
That you call on me to check on me
That you sent me flowers today
That you cherish all of our love
That you meet me halfway everyday
That you love me for who I am
That I love you for who you are
That soon we'll build a family
That soon we'll tie the knot
It's so beautiful because I know I want to spend the rest
of my life with you
It's beautiful because you're the one my heart belongs to
Beautiful you are
Beautiful we are
Yes, this is us
So beautiful

That's My Man

I seen you walk by the way
You looked my way
Even today I'm grateful that I have you
I love you
See when I think on our love
Tears fall to my eyes then I begin to smile
I smile because I dream about you
I smile because I talk about you
I smile because I can't be without you
I smile because I respect you
I smile because you are the one
The one who completes me
The one who loves me
The one who is there for me
The one who doesn't hurt me
The one who motivates me
The one who cares for me
The one who works hard for our family
The one who always makes me happy
The one who kisses me even when my hair is nappy
The one who rather see me live my dreams
The one who makes my sun shine
The one whose love comes once in a lifetime
The one who holds my hand
Yes, that's my man

Only Dreaming?

Dream big
Work harder

The thing is many dreamed but never to plan to make it their reality

Even if it's seeing my best friend living his dream or
seeing my own dream right in front of me

Truth be told, you don't have to just dream, you want it, go get it
Take it

Chasing dreams was never meant to be easy but believing in yourself
    will get you far and having faith is key
There comes a time when your dreams become reality and it's up to you
    work hard and and stay true to yourself

Whoever said that your dream was just a dream you dreamed
It's not
Work hard, it becomes reality
To answer your question, no you're not only dreaming

Many Don't Know

Many don't know how real life is
Many don't know what love is
Many don't know who God is
Many don't know what real is
Many don't know how genuine I feel when I write this poem
Many don't know how to motivate thy self and stop hatin' on the next
Many won't ever get up out the hood
Many will
Many will kill just for the next couple dollars
Many will rob for various reasons
Many will let love take over their mind
And many will read this and probably not give a fuck

What many should realize is keep ya eyes on your prize, keep the flame
      built up and someday you could be something
You can't be anything if you never try
Sometimes you gotta cry and keep movin'

Many are the world, in the end, you, you and, I are the world

Hard Life

Many can't stress enough that the place they stand in life is a miracle

Born to a mother that was addicted to the crack
Born to a daddy that was addicted to cash

They're dealing with real life problems at young ages
No matter what, they'll continue to move forward
They were taken from their homes
Foster care didn't care about them

Mama go to rehab
Daddy around
Mama and daddy separate

Mama got a new man
Know how it feels to watch your mother cry and scared to get out of bed
    and help because you feared he will kill you?
Hearing the screams and hits

Know how it feels?

No, see you don't and you probably never will
They got older and grew up with the minds of a rebel

So when they choose to ignore the negativity, appreciate it and realize
    they're trying to make a difference

They're from the family of the hard knocks

The place they may stand is a miracle and oh this just the beginning
Admire their differences and cherish them
They could have been tomorrow's assassins or the burglar at your door
Accept them because they have made it through a hard life

I Have Risen

I will still stand in the darkest moments even if in that moment, I
     become depress
That's the strength in me, I'm that strong
If they drag me down in the dirt, I will come up cleaner

To be all I can be is my focus
To be real at all times, I shall remain
I have to watch my back because people ain't what they portray to be

To keep the work ethic and believe in myself is all I remain to do
To try to be a civilized young person is my mind state

Knowing there's nothing I can't do is my mind state
So ambitious mistaken to be conceited

Just smile when they talk down on me is all I will do
To continue to excel in every possible way is what I must thrive to do
To reach for the stars is what I will do, driven
I have risen

Ready To Die

You gotta live everyday like it's ya last

Thinkin' on when you will die

See I'm ready now because that's the type of attitude you gotta have
        when you don't know anything

If I knew when I would die, I would prepare for it

The preparation of my death is to keep livin' like it my last, and work
        hard to complete the task God gave me for his purpose for putting
        me on Earth

The preparation for my death is for those who I loved dearly to
        remember me right

If I shall die, my spirits shall live on thru you

I woke up feelin' like I don't have much time to do what I'm destined to
        do
So I live making plans that if I shall live the next day

I'm not scared to die
We all have to, but moral of this poem is to make the best of life while
        you have it
Cause' it's a short trip

Just remember it's short trip, so get a grip on ya destiny

Protect Me

Protect me from those who rise up against me
Protect me from failure that tries to win me
Protect me from this cold and messed up world
Protect me from the violence that comes about
Protect me from the bloody men
Protect me from a broken heart
Protect me and correct me if necessary
Protect me and save me from all dangers
Protect me so that I may fly and not fall
Protect me from the dangers of society
Protect me from all the harm of the wild
Protect me and help to rise again and again

There's A Bigger Picture

Although words have been spoken and things have been said
Times got rough
Times were good
I will always be here for you and them
I made an oath to always keep it real
I started off with you
I will stick through with it
I keep my word, my word is everything
We might not even talk but I do know that I still care and you'll always
      be loved
Life is too short to get mad, let's be through with that
I love you all because how could I even get mad at the biggest or even
      the little things?
There are other things in the world to be mad at like little kids not able
      to eat, little kids born with diseases
Little kids not even having a home
It's so much more to life than the petty things
See the thing is
Our attitude tends to get in the way but you have to come to your right
      mind and say all this is nonsense
There's a bigger picture
Like the world's poverty or my own hometown in the top 5 for living in
      poverty
There's a bigger picture
Like world hunger, homeless people
The shelters getting over capacity
The hospitals drowned with teen pregnancies
The clinics filled with positivity for HIV
I know someone has got to feel me
It's a bigger picture
Everyone's trying to jack which is really whack when
There's a bigger picture

Yes I Can

You said that I wouldn't make it far in life
I'm far and I'm here
You said I wouldn't be anything in life
I'm somebody
You said people will hate me, well you were right, they do but then like
    you said people
While other people appreciate me and my deeds
I am the future of success

You said that I had no future, Oh my, I have one of the brightest futures
You said I'll be another statistic, but I'm not, I'm history in the making
I'm fearless
I do have a dream and it will be shown and it will come true
I am the person you wish you could be
Yes I can go beyond my hopes and dreams
Yes you can look at it like there's more to life
It's so much more
A lot more, as of this day I can motivate myself to be more than another
    statistic
You should not hate on the next

YOU are those who feel they can't do it, those who down others
Those who envy others
YOU get nowhere hating or downing another person, it's not a safe trip
YOU get nowhere tryin' to be somethin' you aren't
YOU have to believe in yourself, YOU have to believe in all is possible
Nothing's impossible; all you need is faith and stay loyal
Reach for the stars
Yes I can
Yes you can
Yes they can
Yes, we all can make the impossible possible

I'd Rather

I'd rather be single than broken-hearted
I'd rather be a stripper than let you use me
I'd rather be told the truth than a lie
I'd rather go BLIND than see you treat me this way
I'd rather forget you than to go insane
I'd rather take this pain of hurt than to take the pain of being damn
near crazy cause I kept tryna overlook everything

I refuse to cry

I was true to you
Never did I disrespect you
I was by your side
Something told me to cry and I did when I seen them texts but I
believed you when you said she was just a friend and see I loved
you so much so I believed that

I'm sitting here thinking of all the dreams you sold me and the same you
sold to her
I'm glad I cried that time cause this time it ain't no need to cry

I'D RATHER BE SINGLE THAN BROKEN-HEARTED

I'D RATHER GO BLIND THAN TO SEE YOU TREAT ME THIS
WAY

Listen Ladies

WHEN YOU'RE TIRED OF A MAN
LET HIM GO
WHEN YOU'RE BEING THE MAN OF THE HOUSE
LET HIM GO

LEARN YOU HAVE YOU YOURSELF, AND YOU!
ENOUGH IS ENOUGH

WEAK WITHOUT HIM? HELL NAW
SAD, STRESSED, AND DEPRESSED WITHOUT HIM? HELL
    NAW

WOMEN YOU ARE POWERFUL
NO MAN NECESSARY
MOST MEN ARE BOYS AND I'M TELLIN THE TRUTH
CAUSE' WE WOMEN PLAY THE RIGHT ROLE MORE THAN
    WHAT WE'RE WAS SUPPOSE TO, SO WE CAN SAY
    THAT WITH PROOF

LADIES STOP LETTIN' MEN TAKE OVER
IT'S A WOMAN'S WORLD, WOMEN RUN THE WORLD
IF IT WASN'T WOMEN
THE WORLD WOULD NOT GO ROUND!!
LISTEN LADIES
HE WILL BE BACK, HE WILL WANT YOU BACK
YOU TELL HIM EASIER SAID THEN DONE
SHOW IT
DON'T SETTLE FOR LESS THAN YOUR BEST
DON'T RUN WITH DOGS
DO WHAT YOU GOTTA DO FOR YOU
BE SELFISH
PUT YO SELF FIRST!
LADIES LISTEN AND STOP REMINSCING

The One (Don't Hate Me Now)

One who does speak as they feel
One who will die for what's real
One who will stay by your side although things aren't too well
One who will believe in you when you think hope is lost
One who will stand up and decide what's right for thyself

so independent
so mysterious
so responsible
so emotional
so ready for whatever
so modest
so confident
so ambitious

Yes, I'm the one
The one they hate
The one they look up to
The one they admire
The one that does as she desires
The one that will work over time
The one that cannot and will not stop when it comes to achieving her
    dreams
The one that knows exactly what she wants in life
The one who always stay down to Earth
The one who will not settle for the status quo
The one who can be a bit mean
The one who can't save herself from her ambitious ways
The one who knows in the end, it's all gravy

I'm not Tracy McGrady, but I'm the chosen one
So don't hate me now

This Is Why

I'm passionate about whatever I put interest in, however the ambition
    keeps me goin'
Whenever hard work is needed, it's there
Nothing less of the best
I do impress
Many

Friends came and went because of all the ambition
The unthinkable starts happening while in the back of their minds, they
    envy
Smile in ya face and say they happy
It's me that know I have only myself in the end
Why is it that they pretend?
I couldn't tell you why

If I have offended you, not sorry, the truth hurts, love me for having the
    passion to be honest
I've offended you because I excelled the quickest
I've offended you because I work the hardest
I've offended you because I know what I want in life
I've offended you because I won't protect myself using a knife
I've offended you because I don't settle for less
I've offended you because I know I deserve the best
I've offended you because I do things you wish you could
I've offended you because you never thought I would
This is why they can't stand me
This is why I rise
This is why I have lots of haters
This is why I am above my age
This is why I'll achieve all my dreams
This is why I'm so blessed
Yes
This is why

It's Not Hard, Better Yet It's Easier

To get a job
To shine like oil
To walk with a pep in ya step
To be so damn cocky
To be so real
To get respect by the time this poem ends
To make it in this life
To stand by your word
To be in love
To stay in love
To ride or die
like I said it's not hard, better yet it's easier

Than
Sittin' and doin' nothin'
Low self esteem
Wasting time and hatin'
Wasting time and talkin' about what you ain't
Walkin' with guilt on ya shoulder
To be so not confident
To be fake
or just to do you
It's not hard, better yet it's easier

I make my decisions to the fullest of my intensions so everything is for a
        reason
You talk it, try walkin' it
I'm livin' for me while wearing my crown
I hope all the hatin' simmers down
It's not hard, better yet easier!

This Love

This love is AMAZING!
This love seem sad at times
This love is stressful and hard at times
This love is CONSTANTLY hated on
This love is talked about OFTEN
This love is wished on
This love have no limit
This love is serious
This love is real
This love is meant to be
This love is random but seemed to be lasting forever
This love is a bit irritating sometimes
This love is so true
The love is riding or dying
This love is frowns and smiles
This love is ready for up and downs and has been thru ups and downs
This love is complicated sometimes
This love is spoken to be us
This love is what explains me and you

Beyond Love

From the time we met, I was sure that I could never see the end, at least
not yet
Something so strong, something so real, something very efficient,
something like we're meant makes me stay so true to you
Never said this love would be easy, never said we're something like a
fairytale
Just know one thing's for sure is that you love me something I can tell
More than just friends till the end, more than just my man
More like my lifetime partner and true friend till the very end
What I feel for you is beyond love
What I live for and see in you is beyond love
I guess I got myself in this situation of being so soaked in your love
To spend my life with you is indeed the greatest ride, yet my favorite
To be the one for you is like a dream come true, more than anything
else, I love that fact that what we have is so real and true
Better yet, words that's permanent to my heart is I love you
I swear this feeling is beyond love

I Don't Understand

I'm supposed to understand why you do the things you do?
I'm supposed to understand why you aren't as affectionate as me?
I'm supposed to understand why I hold you down thru all your
wrongdoing?
I'm supposed to understand why I let you treat me this way?
I'm supposed to forget the lies, pains, and hurts?
Will I ever feel like this is it, you're the one?
See, it's a mind over matter situation, something like a catch 22, I'm
not sure what to do, all I know is to hold on and keep goin' strong. I
can't let go, of my word, of you, of our love, of what we have. Do you
feel the same? Sometimes I feel so shame especially when I know you
called me out my name, see some things most of us women could never
understand why we accept so much from these men. Most of us women
don't really know why we take so much. In thee end, we are the true
riders, we are the soul survivors, and we are the real ones.

Never Knew

I never knew someone who broke the heart can put it back together
I never knew someone could lie to someone just not to hurt them when
we all know what's in the dark comes to light
I never knew I would hold on so tight to a love that seem so right
I never will know how much he cares because he really doesn't share his
thoughts, his love, his true feelings
I never will know if I'll ever really be happy with him, all I know is I'm
sticking to my word no matter what
I never knew that I was so full of resentment
I never knew what I really felt until you were gone
I never knew that you actually cared
I never knew you actually loved me
I never knew he needed me as much as I needed him
I kinda knew you were heaven sent though
Here's just some things I wanna know, can you hold my hand? In life, in
everything I do, in success, in stress, in my wellness, in my deepest fears,
even in my tears, in my dreams, in my nightmares, and in my fantasies?
I never knew how much I admire you and needed you

All I Know

All I know is that I'm suppose to ride until the very end
All I know is I'm tired of getting dragged in the dirt
All I know is I must not be tired because I keep forgiving him
All I know is he says he needs me, then why intentionally do wrong?
All I know is he says he loves me, but lies to me
All I know is if he lies; on the bottom of my foot is where his name will
     lie
All I know is if he hurts me, sorry forever is what he'll be
All I know is if you love me, show it
All I know is words don't mean anything, but actions mean more than
     something
All I know is if you tryna use me, watch what I do
All I know is if you don't really love me, I'm leaving
All I know is if you care for me, you would try to do better
All I know is if I keep taking you back, you'll never understand where
     I'm coming from
Oh, so you hear me now?
So you feel me now?
You love me now?
You care for me now?
 Yea, you mad now?
Oh you know I'm talkin' about you now?
All I know is I'm smarter than you think
All I know is I'm every woman that goes through the same things,
     trying to be there for these men, and then they don't act right
All I know is you better get right, or else to the opposite of the right
All I feel is this love may be worth the fight

What Does It Mean?

When you say you love me?
When you say you would die for me?
When you say everything all gravy?
When you say you gon' hold me down?
When you lie for no reason?
When you hold me tightly?
When you keep me around?
When you use me?
When you hit me?
When you take a bullet for me?
When you put it all on the line for me?
When you talk to other people?
When you say they mean nothing?
When you look me in my eye and lie?
When you say you don't want to be with anyone else?
When you say you need me?
When you say you will never leave me?
When you drag me in the dirt?
Seriously what does all this mean? It means some of the men we talk to
    aren't whose they portray to be
These men aren't as real as they claim to be
These men aren't really supporting us
These men aren't really caring for us, if anything they stressin' us
If anything they're after us, after us to make us feel miserable just like
    them
These men are stupid, so they want us to be stupid with them by arguing
    back or fighting back
These are the men we choose to date, the men that we love to hate
These are indeed some of the men that hold us back especially when
    we're black
These are the men we take so much from
What does this mean?

The Black Society

You rather see me on my back
Feedin' a newborn similac
Then see me workin' hard, givin' my all, yet standin' tall
Why is it that the black society hate amongs each other?
Why can't we love one another?
Why can't we hold hands?
Maybe even be friends
See you rather see less progress then success
You rather have a gang of killas
Callin' each other niggas
Really?
That's the real us?
That's what's hot?
Naw, it's not
You rather sit back and be broke
When's there's no more Welfare, you already sayin' it ain't fair,see a lot of
        us gon' choke
When it's gone
Life ain't a joke
We're pure and oh so strong
Remember when we were slaves waitin' to be free?
Oh, you forgot huh?
Or is it just me knowing that we're put on Earth to be all we can be
Yet you rather kill for the next dollar bill
What happened to the black society?

When I Look Back

I could have been dead
I could have been beaten
I could have been pregnant
I could have been crazy
I could have been wild
I could have lost my mind
I could have went astray
I could have lost my way
No weapon formed against me shall prosper
God will never leave you nor give you a load too heavy
God will never leave your side
When I look back at all the things I could have been or done
I get excited because if it wasn't for God, I would not be where I am in
      life now
Never lose your faith because God you can always hold on to
One question for you
Without God, where would you be?
When you look back
When they look back
When I look back

You're So Dumb

You left an independent woman for a dependent girl
You left a young lady with credentials for someone with no potential, yet
      so simple
You left a young lady with multiple incomes for someone with no
      income
You left someone who has her head on right for someone who head
      screwed on wrong
You left a girl with potential who is professional for one without smarts
      and is ghetto
You are so damn stupid
You said you needed space, very funny
How could you not want to be committed to someone who has it all
      versus someone who is part of the percentage of clueless?
You're so dumb
You are the man who leaves paradise for the slums
You are the man that wants to be a whore instead of settling when
      everything you asked for is right in front of you
You are the man who claims to be real, yet fake
You are the man who really thrives to be hard, yet soft
You are the man that wants to make moves, but stand still
You are the man who says his word is everything, but lie about anything
You are the man who's very dumb
You are the man that thinks I'll wait for you
You are the man who will always run back, but eventually running back
      won't help you
You are the man I could destroy, but will not
You are the man that always says sorry because you're sorry
You are the man who is confuse and made the decision to lose
You are the man who won't have as much as others
You are the man who I wrote this poem about
You are the man who is so dumb, no doubt

"This Is What It Is"

I been here all of along
I stayed around even when you felt all alone
I had your back even when no one else did
You get released from jail
Nice and actin' right for a few months
Back to the basics
You said you cared
You didn't
You said you weren't lying but you were
You said she meant nothin' but she does
You said that it was me and you but really it was a lie
You said you loved me, not in love
Read between the lines
No I read between the lies
I'm using what I read between the lines because now it's colder
You ain't nothin'
You are not who you say you are
You are the liar that broke the heart
You are the liar that pain is numb to
You are the liar I just don't care for anymore
You are the liar that I must erase from my life
Yes, I am indeed dedicating this to you
Every liar that have sat and lived a lie
Every liar that have broken the innocent's heart
This is what it is

A Lasting Crush

I was just vibin' to
The music of the party
Then I was introduce to you
Who knew I would be so attracted to you
Now that was the first time
Saturday night, we meet once again under the dimmed light
I see a loving, caring, respectful, and honest man with potential
You're so worthy
Maybe someday you could be my king and I'll be your loyal queen
Third time around
I'm really attracted now
You left me in suspense
We talked a bit more
What is it that I sense?
Something like a rush or
A Lasting Crush

Dear The Younger Version of Me

I miss you because you were a rock that never cried
I resent you because crying releases the pain and you didn't shed a tear
I miss you because you were so heartless
I resent you because now you have too much heart
I miss you because you never took disrespect
I resent you because now you just take all disrespect
I applaud you because you're on your way
I applaud you because you know there's more to life
I applaud you because you will be somebody
I applaud you because you got your diploma
I applaud you because you know the sky is the limit
I applaud you because you took the disadvantages and use them to your
    advantage
I applaud you because you didn't let others get in the way of your
    destination
I applaud you because you didn't let anyone tell you no
You're unstoppable
I applaud you because you're leaving your mark that will not and cannot
    be erased
Dear The Younger Version of me,
Are you proud of me?

It Didn't Hurt
(At Least Not This Time)

When the phone call was received, I just snapped back
When threats were made, I just laid back
No need to react, just fade to black
When I realized you lied, I laughed
It would be a shame if I'd cried
I know I tried, tried to be there and always around
Sometimes you got let things go, go ahead and be with the hoe
In the end, you'll be back, never waiting, just anticipating in what I need
      to do for me
I didn't need you, you were dead weight
I look real good now huh?
I didn't need you, I made myself believe that, how whack
I wasn't in love with you, more like trying to be there for you
They say when you love someone
You just don't treat him bad
Now how sad, all of this because you were mad
Sorry won't work, whenever I forgive you, I will not be in love with you
I will always have love for you, friends till the end
See this time, it didn't hurt
I'm good and living life just like I should
One last thing, it didn't hurt, at least not this time

All Thee Ifs

If I wasn't dragged in the dirt, would I really be successful?
If I wasn't beaten, would I even know how to defend myself?
If I wasn't ever bullied, would I even be able to stand up?
If life was easy, would I still work hard?
If I was unemployed, would I give up?
If I was another race, would I be as bold?
If I was a boy, would I act like them?
If I was rich, would I be a bitch?
If I was hell proof, would I pray?
If I got fired today, would my mind state go astray?
If this reader read this, would they do some thinking?

Still Innocent

Through all of the heartbreaks
Through all of the name calling
Through all of the wrong doing
Through all of the pain
Through all of the lack of respect

Through all of the lies
Through all of the hurt
Through all your growth
Through all of your rhymes
Throughout your lifetime
Young boy, still trying to find your way
Still tryna find himself
Still trying to understand this thing called life
Still don't really know what you want
Lost in this world
No matter how bad it hurts
No matter the reoccurrences of the same hurt
No matter the tears I cried
No matter the pain I felt
No matter the harsh words you used
No matter how much you never cared
You're still innocent
Innocent because of the young boy I met
Innocent because I know I have your heart
Innocent because I know you'll come back
Innocent because you've been through a lot
Innocent because I trust in you
Innocent because you're gifted
Innocent because you're wrong doing is in recovery
Yes, in my heart, you'll still innocent
In the flesh, you're an innocent
Still innocent

The Time Invested

So many tears throughout the years
So many feelings and emotions
The ride got rough
The ride gets rough
The vibe gets bad then good
The vibe got sad then mad
What I'm telling you is yes, this is real
What I'm telling you this is love that we're meant
What I'm telling you is that love has come our way
What I'm telling you is I will hold on tight
We'll be alright because of the time invested
The time invested in us, us as in you and me

Better Run

From the one who broke your heart
From the one who didn't care about you
From the one you went hard for
From the one you remained loyal to
From the one you never would disrespect
From the one who hit you
From the one you did time for
From the one whom you stole for
From the one whom you always came through for
See the one, will not harm you in no way or form
The one will not lie to you
The one will not hit you
The one will not take you for granite
The one will not anyone disrespect you
The one will stay down with you through all the struggles
The one will be there for you through all the ups and downs
The one will seek something good
The one will have the mind state I wish somebody would, especially
        when it comes to you
The one is the only one you can always depend on
The one is your rock
What I'm sayin' is you're not the one because you all the chaos you've
        done
Only thing left to do is realize you're not the one, so I better run

I Can See Your Halo

All of the support
All of the love
All of the care
All of the advice
All of the hugs
All of the kisses
All of the time
The times that got bad
The times that got real sad
The times that were good
All this time you been around
The way you stayed down
The way you told me to wear my crown
How you told me to keep my eyes on the prize
How you always have my back
How you told me drama was whack
How you didn't discriminate me because I'm black
How you always said the sweetest things
How you always keep it real
How you always told me to say what I feel
How you always remained my rock
Indeed you told me I was a woman who really rocked
Indeed you told me that we ride until the end of time
Indeed you told me that you would never leave
Indeed you told me you loved me
Indeed you told me how proud of me you were of me
Indeed you told me to shake off the haters
Back then I could not see what you seen in me
Back then I could not see that light
That light over your head
That light in your eyes
That light that shines thru your heart
That light in your arms
That light in your voice
That light in your willing

It's been a long time and I can say truly
I can see your halo

What's Best?

For us to depart
For us to call it quits
For me to get over you
For me to let you go completely
For me to get out of this circle
For me to actually put me first
For me to take care of me
For me to go solo and on my own
For me to just not look for love anymore
For me to just wait patiently
For me to love me for me
For me to excel in school
For me to never to accept no when it comes to my ambitions
For me to know I will rise again after the downfall
To look out for me
To live for the moment
To accept change
To live my dream
To show love to my team
To realize that it's my life
Yes, this is what's best, what's best for me

I'll Still Stand

Even if no one else have my back
Even if my family leave
Even if my friends go astray
Even if my mind zone far away
I'll still stand
Even if I have to travel alone
Even if times get rough
Even if I have no shoulder to lean on
Even if the world becomes hectic
I'll still stand
Even in my fears
Even in my worst nightmares
Even in my worries
Even in my dreams
Even in reality
Even in a fantasy
I'll still stand
I'll stand because I have to
I'll stand for those who weren't able to
I'll stand for those who aren't as true to confidence
I'll stand for those who don't care
I'll stand for those who try
I'll stand for those who cry
I'll stand with a complete alibi
I'll always seek a way to stand
One thing I cannot do is not stand
So thru it all, I'll still stand

If I Were These Boys

I would not cheat
I would not be so selfish
I would not take my woman for granite
I would not lie so damn much
What would I do if I were these boys?
I would treat my woman right
I would give her unconditional love
I would be loyal to her
I would stand up for her, not front on her
I would give her all of me
I would keep it real with her
I would put no one before her
Why would I do such things?
I love this woman
I want to walk this woman down the aisle
I don't want to hurt this woman
I want to do right by this woman
But if I were these boys in this century, I would show them what a real
    man is
See women, these boys don't care
They don't even listen
They want us women to stay by their side and ride, stay faithful but it's
    not mutual
These boys don't understand what it means to be a real man
These boys don't understand what it means to treat a woman right
To every boy that don't treat these women right, it will come back on
    you

Yeah You Know

That I did graduate
That I did get great jobs
That I did publish this book
That I did stay on my grind
That I did win that battle
That I did excel in my education
That I did do everything you said I couldn't
That I did rock that show
That I did go down in history
See you actin' like you don't know
You
You are the person that tried to hold me back
You are the person that told me no
You are the person that told me it could not happen
You are the person that told me that I could not win
You are the person that told me I could not make it without you
You are the person that I did make it with out
You are the person that hated on me
Notice I see
Notice I analyze
Notice that I flourish
Notice that I continue to survive
Notice that I still stay on top
Notice that I laugh at all the negativity
Notice I gain prosperity
Notice I do go hard
I just have one thing to say to You
Yeah you know!

They Just Ain't Real

For the moment, they love you
For the moment, they support you
For the moment, they wanna be there for you
For the moment, they would do anything for you
For the moment, they would even take a bullet for you
Those people ain't real
In the midst of changes
They talk about you
They laugh at you
They wish badly upon you
They're glad you're goin' through it
They are not happy for you
They will do anything to break you
I promise you, your surroundings ain't always true
They just ain't real
They're seasonal, their demeanors change throughout the seasons
They use you when you're hot
They'll abuse you when you're cold
They'll be amused when you fail
They just ain't real

How Life Changed

Now they love me
Now they want to be me
Now they talk bad about me
Now they wish they were me
Now they acknowledge me
Now they judge me
Now they would do anything to take me out
Now they admire me
Now they cherish me
Now they see me
Now they understand me
Now they feel I'm so worthy
Now I see how in that one moment
How life changed

The Life You Chose

It's up to you, you made a decision
You made that decision to live that way
You made that decision to just do you
You made that decision to turn to who you want to
You made that decision to turn to drugs
You made that decision to strip at that club
You made that decision to deal with domestic violence
You made that decision to resort to violence
You made that decision to rob them innocent people
You made that decision to let negativity get to you, now you fightin'
You made that decision to lose your rights
You made that decision to do their time
You can't blame someone else for the decision you made, you did that
You chose your own life
You chose to live that way
You can't get mad because you chose the life you chose
Yes this is the life
The life you chose

You Can't Forget

What our ancestors went through
What our parents went through
What you went through to get where you are
You cannot forget how much hard work you put in
How you didn't let the negativity get in
You cannot forget how much time you have invested
You cannot forget how much you love what you do
Cannot forget what your dreams are
Cannot forget that the world is yours
Cannot forget that you were born to be all you can
Cannot forget how much you tried
Cannot forget how much you cried
No don't forget that there is time
Time to adjust
Time to express
Time for success
No time for stress
Get it all off your chest
You cannot forget that you did try your best

Feel My Pain

The cruel words
The harsh hits
The heavy tears
The temptation to hurt myself
The low self esteem
The crazy diets
The shameful moments
The embarrassment
The hatred
The resentment
Did you listen to me?
Did you love me?
Did you care about me?
You are the person that made me feel so shitty
You are the person I could not escape
You are the person I still have to face up to this day
You are the person that made my life so fuckin' miserable
You are the person that hurted me so badly
Mentally
Physically
All the pain I felt and I'm so young
All the tears I cried, damn near drowned
All the words you killed me with
All the times I was neglected
All the times I didn't matter
All the times you never cared
Yes, I was mistreated
Mistreat me
Mistreat them
Mistreat us
Feel their pain
Feel our pain
Feel my pain

Lonely

Never had anyone
Never could talk to anyone
Never could love anyone
Never could even love myself
Alone at this crossroad
Alone at this side road
Alone in this life
Alone in my dreams
Alone in my reality
Lonely, no one to depend on
Lonely, because I have nowhere to go
Lonely, because I don't know who to trust
Lonely, because I didn't feel that my own loved me
This life could so lonely
Am I the only that's lonely

No Real Family

These people talk about us
These people judge us
These people embarrass us
These people beat us
These people made us feel like shit
These people told us we could not do it
These people didn't care for us
These people didn't motivate us
These people wish the worse for us
These people try to break us
These people can't wait to see us fall
These people just ain't beautiful
These people fight us
These people would kill us
This is my family?
The family that suppose to care right?
The family that suppose to love us right?
The family that suppose to be there for us right?
The family that should accept our flaws?
No real family

My Own Motivation

I will not stop, gotta keep workin my way to the top
I will not keep my head down, gotta stand up to put on my crown
I will not lose my way at least not today
I'll thrive
I'll strive
I will continue to dive into my dreams
See, I don't need a hater
See, I don't need a man
See, I don't need a friend
See, I don't need anyone
I'm my own inspiration
I get myself lifted because I know I'm gifted
I get myself inspired, because I can make it thru the wire
Inspired off what I know I can be
Inspired off knowing the world is mine
Inspiration, yes I am my own motivation

About the Author

Rachel Greer was born in Milwaukee, Wisconsin, she was raised there also. In her teen years, she loved to recite Maya Angelou poems in the after school activity of Forensics. Her favorite poem to recite was, ***Phenomenal Woman*** by Maya Angelou. She loved the confidence Ms.Angelou had. Rachel strives everyday to be the phenomenal young woman that she is. Rachel attended a suburban school in the state of Wisconsin. She managed to graduate 1 year early from high school and pushed on to college. She currently attends a technical school in her area with desires to earn an Associate's Degree in Business Management. While being a freshman in college, she has the title of a Wisconsin Scholar. Rachel is naturally ambitious, she looks for more ways to back up her mission and that's building an empire before she dies. Rachel feels she has a purpose for being put on Earth and everyone she will touch in some way or form. Rachel enjoys working, shopping, school, and real guys. As she would say, "I'm a robot, but still a bit normal." Rachel is a woman of her word, yet very dedicated to everything she's involved in. In Rachel's eyes, if you have faith and stay loyal; nothing's impossible and that way you may reach for the stars. This young woman really believes that the world is hers, and you only lose if you choose. One thing that makes her stand out is the fact that she won't let anyone tell her no when it comes to her ambitions and dreams. At this moment of time she says, she feels so alive. Rachel is indeed grasping every bit of her destiny. ***Words of Inspiration from Your Own Kind*** is yet her proudest accomplishment.